# Rhinos

Victoria Blakemore

Copyright info/picture credits

Cover, JONATHAN PLEDGER/Shutterstock; Page 3, hansbenn/ Pixabay; Page 5, kdsphotos/Pixabay; Page 7, skeeze/Pixabay; Page 9, ronbd/Pixabay; Pages 10-11, MonikaP/Pixabay; Page 13, ronbd/Pixabay; Page 15, Storyblocks; Page 17, Gellinger/ Pixabay; Page 19, Lienve/Pixabay; Page 21, hehlich/Pixabay; Page 23; splongo/Pixabay; Page 25, Storyblocks; Page 27, Pexels/Pixabay; Page 29, MonikaP/Pixabay; Page 31, Moni-kaP/Pixabay;  Page 33, JONATHAN PLEDGER/Shutterstock

# Table of Contents

# What Are Rhinos?

Rhinoceroses, or rhinos, are large mammals known for the horns on their snouts. They are related to animals such as tapirs and horses.

There are five different kinds of rhinos. They differ in where they live, their color, and what they eat.

Rhinos are usually gray and

brown in color.

# Size

Adult rhinos range in size from six to twelve feet long. They can be up to nearly seven feet tall.

When fully grown white rhinos can weigh over 7,000 pounds. Sumatran rhinos are usually closer to 1,000 pounds.

Male rhinos are usually larger

and heavier than female rhinos.

# Physical Characteristics

Rhinos have a thick, tough skin. It helps to protect them from the sun. It can also help to protect them from predators.

Rhino horns are made from **keratin**. They can be used to dig up roots to eat. They are also used for self defense.

The Sumatran rhino, black rhino, and white rhino all have two large horns. The Javan and Indian rhino only have one horn.

# Habitat

Rhinos live in savannas, swamps, and forests, where there are plenty of plants to eat.

They live in very warm **climates** and are often found close to a water source, such as a river or lake.

# Range

Rhinos are found in southern

Africa and Asia.

10

They are often seen in countries like South Africa, Kenya, India, and Zimbabwe.

# Diet

Rhinos are **herbivores**, which means that they eat only plants.

Most rhinos eat leaves and fruit. White rhinos feed mainly on grasses. They do most of their feeding early in the morning and at night, when it is cooler.

Rhinos don't have very good eyesight. They use their sense of smell to find food.

# Predators

Adult rhinos do not have many predators, but young rhinos are prey for a number of other animals.

Crocodiles, wild dogs, and hyenas have all been known to attack young rhinos.

Rhinos can use their horns to

protect themselves and young

rhinos from predators.

15

# Communication

Rhinos use scent, sound, and movement to communicate.

They can make sounds such as squeals, grunts, snorts, and growls.

Rhinos can mark their territory using their **waste**. It tells other rhinos to stay away.

Rhinos flatten their ears against their head as a warning. They may rub up against other rhinos to show affection.

# Movement

Rhinos can run fast when they need to. Some have been **observed** running at speeds of up to thirty-five miles per hour for short distances.

They are able to turn quickly. This helps them when they are defending themselves or their calves from predators.

Most of the time, rhinos do not

run. They walk or trot to move

from place to place.

# Rhino Calves

Rhinos usually have one baby, or calf. Calves stay with their mothers for about two years.

When calves are first born, they are covered with hair. It helps to keep them warm and prevent sunburn.

Rhino mothers are very **protective**

of their calves. They keep them

safe from predators.

# Rhino Life

Most rhinos are **solitary**, which means that they live alone. They are thought to be shy and keep to themselves.

Rhinos tend to be **aggressive**. They may attack people or other animals who get too close. They rarely attack unless they are **provoked**.

Rhinos spend a lot of their time

awake grazing and looking for

food.

# Staying Cool

Since rhinos live in places where it is very hot, they can overheat. There are a few ways they can keep cool.

Rhinos roll around in the mud. The mud hardens on their body and works as a sunscreen. It helps them to stay cool.

Some rhinos rest when the day

is too hot. They look for food

when it is cooler.

All rhino species are **endangered** or **critically endangered**. There are not many left in the wild.

There are thought to be fewer than one hundred Sumatran and Javan rhinos left in the wild.

In the wild, rhinos can live

about thirty-five years.

# Rhinos in Danger

Rhinos are facing several threats. They are often hunted for their horns, which are used in medicines and for decoration.

In some places, rhino populations have been hunted so much that they are too spread out. This makes it hard for populations to increase.

Their habitats are also being

destroyed for farmland,

buildings, and roads.

# Helping Rhinos

There are several ways that people are trying to help rhinos. Special **preserves** have been set up to provide animals like rhinos with a safe habitat.

These preserves are often **patrolled** by rangers who watch for **poachers**.

In many countries, it is **illegal** to hunt rhinos. In other countries, it is **illegal** to bring rhino horns or bones into the country.

Some groups work to educate people about rhinos. They hope that people will want to help if they know more about them.

# Glossary

**Aggressive:** likely to attack

**Climate**: the usual weather in a

particular place

**Critically Endangered**: nearly extinct

**Endangered**: at risk of becoming extinct

**Herbivore**: an animal that eats only

plants

**Illegal**: against the law

**Keratin**: the protein that makes up

human nails and hair

**Observed**: seen

**Patrolled:** guarded by taking regular trips through

**Poacher:** someone who hunts animals illegally

**Protective**: likely to protect

**Provoked**: bothered, made angry

**Preserves**: areas of land set up to protect plants and animals

**Solitary**: living alone

**Waste:** material given off by the body after food is digested

# About the Author

Victoria Blakemore is a first grade

teacher in Southwest Florida with a

passion for reading.

You can visit her at

www.elementaryexplorers.com

# Also in This Series

| | | | | | | |
|---|---|---|---|---|---|---|
| Gray Wolves | Sloths | Flamingos | Camels | Koalas | Honey Bees | Pandas |
| Pangolins | White-Tailed Deer | Orcas | Giraffes | Corn | Meerkats | Echidnas |
| Walruses | Raccoons | Bald Eagles | Apples | Arctic Foxes | Red Pandas | Cassowaries |
| Tigers | Ladybugs | Moose | Beluga Whales | Leopards | Elephants | Jellyfish |
| Binturongs | Lions | Dolphins | Reindeer | Hammerhead Sharks | Hippos | Pumpkins |
| Peafowl | Chameleons | Florida Panthers | Aye-Ayes | Black Bears | Cheetahs | Manatees |
| Gingerbread | Polar Bears | Hot Chocolate | Orangutans | Coyotes | Marshmallows | Strawberries |

Elementary Explorers

Victoria Blakemore

# Also in This Series

| | | | | | | |
|---|---|---|---|---|---|---|
| Aardvarks | Mako Sharks | Alligators | Frogs | Hedgehogs | Brown Bears | Bongos |
| Sea Turtles | Quokkas | Muskrats | Zebras | Red Foxes | Ring-Tailed Lemurs | Platypuses |
| Anteaters | Kangaroos | Rhinos | Jaguars | Wombats | Capybaras | Gorillas |
| Cats | Skunks | Butterflies | Dingoes | Snow Leopards | African Wild Dogs | Penguins |
| Whale Sharks | Wolverines | Warthogs | Caracals | Badgers | Seals | Hummingbirds |
| Pikas | Humpback Whales | Pumas | Lemonade | Llamas | Tulips | Ostriches |
| Sunflowers | Fennec Foxes | Sea Lions | | | | |

All titles by Victoria Blakemore

Elementary Explorers

www.ingramcontent.com/pod-product-compliance
Lightning Source LLC
Chambersburg PA
CBHW051253020426
42333CB00025B/3191